Contents

What is Music Tracks?	2
What are Small Group Tracks?	3
The exam at a glance	4
Group A Film Music!	5
Vesper's Valse	9
Midnight Carnival	13
English Waltz	17
Group B - Technical Pieces	
Pizzicato Delicato	21
Who Needs Scales?	25
The Musicianship Skills tests - Copyback	29
Copyback - Example 1	30
Copyback - Example 2	31
The Musicianship Skills tests - Improvising	33
Improvising - Example 1	34
Improvising - Example 2	35
CD track listing	36

Published by
Trinity College London

E music@trinitycollege.com
www.trinitycollege.com

Cover and book design by as creatives
Brand development by Alistair Crane
Audio produced and mixed by Ross Power (RP Music), Terl Bryant and Matt Hay
Tracks arranged by composers and Mike Simpson, Alice Hall, Nick Powlesland

Registered in the UK
Company no. 02683033
Charity no. 1014792

Copyright © 2014 Trinity College London

Unauthorised photocopying is illegal
No part of this publication may be copied or reproduced in any
form or by any means without the prior permission of the publisher.
Printed in England by Halstan, Amersham, Bucks.

Small Group Tracks Violin - Track 2   1

What is Music Tracks?

Music Tracks is a programme for young musicians who learn in whole-class and small-group environments. It aims to inspire them, right from when they first pick up an instrument, to explore the work of musicians and composers from the world around them. It promotes creative and collaborative music-making through exciting repertoire and resources, setting young learners on the road to becoming lifelong music-makers.

Music Tracks is made up of two strands:

First Access Track is a package of materials supporting whole-class instrumental and vocal teaching. It includes a wide range of original music, backing tracks and resources.

Small Group Tracks are exams and resources for small-group learning. They are designed to follow on from First Access Track, but are equally suitable for learners who did not begin their learning through First Access Track.

This book supports Small Group Tracks at Track 2 level. It contains everything needed to prepare for and take a Track 2 Small Group Track exam, and has been designed as a useful resource for small-group teaching.

Find out more about Music Tracks at www.trinitycollege.com/musictracks

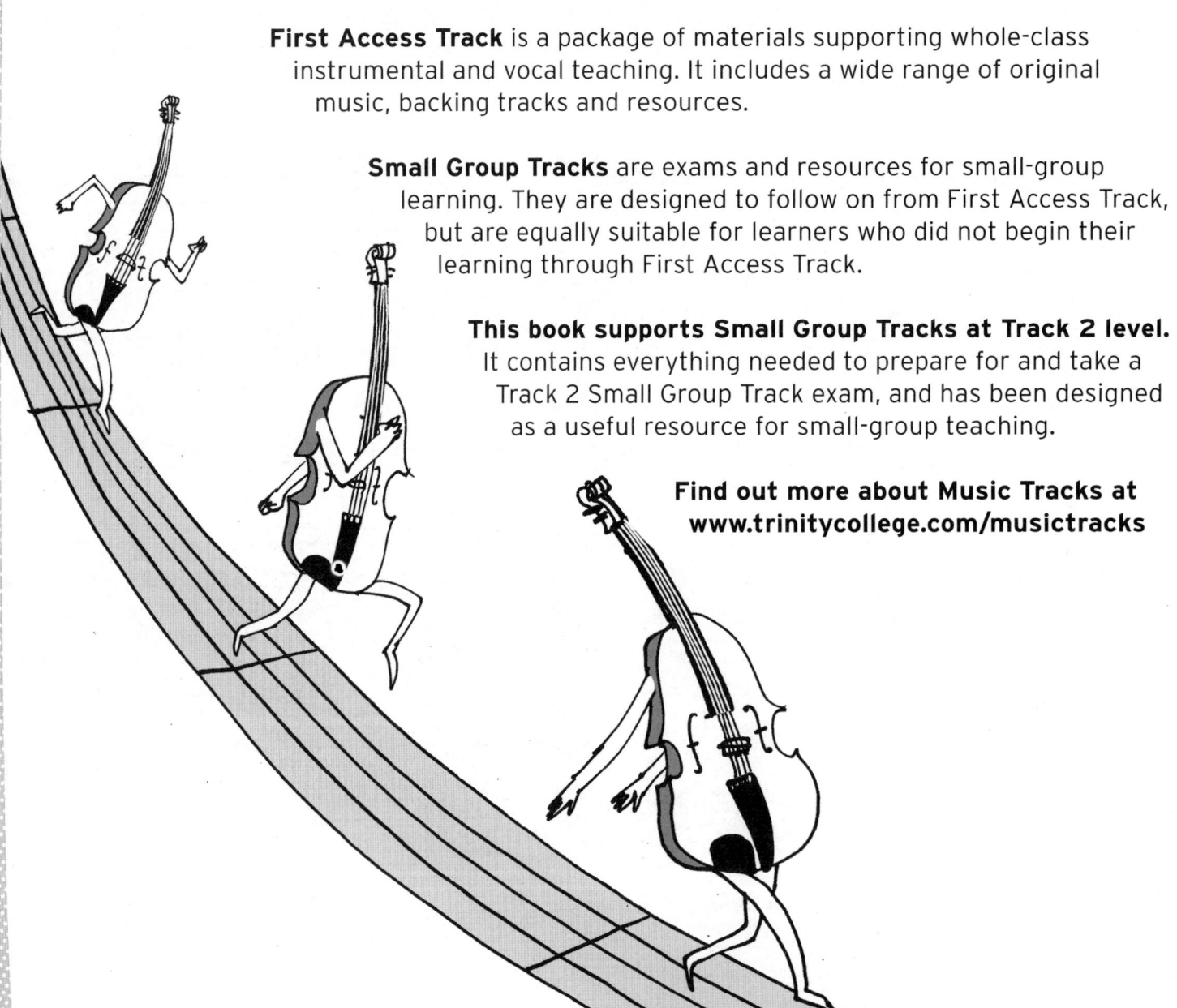

2 Trinity College London

What are Small Group Tracks?

Small Group Tracks are exams and resources for small-group learning. The exams are taken in groups of two to four learners, each of whom is featured as a solo performer in every section of the exam. The learners are assessed by a specially trained Music Tracks examiner, and each receives their own certificate and report form. Supporting resources are provided in a series of Small Group Tracks books, designed to integrate with small-group learning strategies in order to promote holistic musical development.

The exam

Exams are offered at three different levels: Initial, Track 1 and Track 2 (equivalent to Initial, Grade 1 and Grade 2), supporting carefully graded musical progression. In the exam, the group plays three pieces from the relevant Small Group Tracks book, including one Technical Piece. The group also performs one Musicianship Skills test, either Copyback or Improvising. Each learner is assessed as an individual, receiving comments and marks relating to their own performance.

The music

The music draws on styles and genres from around the world and from different periods. Most of the pieces are original compositions, and many include lyrics to encourage aural development through singing or speaking. The pieces in Group A include ensemble and solo sections, allowing learners to demonstrate both types of playing. The pieces in Group B – the Technical Pieces – require learners to take it in turns to play phrases, showing that they understand shape and structure. These pieces also focus on specific technical elements.

The resources

As well as containing everything needed to prepare for the exam, each Small Group Tracks book is packed with ideas and material for small-group teaching, supporting a varied curriculum of learning. Each piece is accompanied by a high-quality backing track, and there is background information on the style of each piece, as well as hints and tips for preparation. Additional resources for teachers and learners are available online – visit www.trinitycollege.com/musictracks for details of how to access these.

The exam at a glance

In the exam, the group performs the following items in the order below:

Piece 1 - a piece from Group A in this book

Piece 2 - a different piece from Group A in this book

Piece 3 - a Technical Piece from Group B in this book

Musicianship Skills - either Copyback or Improvising

Please note that all learners in the group must present the same pieces and Musicianship Skills test. Note also that the repeated section in the Group A pieces must be played as many times as there are learners in the group, so that each learner gets the chance to perform this section as a soloist. All pieces and Musicianship Skills tests are played with a backing track.

Note for teachers

All the pieces in this book have been edited with regard to current performance practice. Dynamics and articulation should be observed except where otherwise stated.

Lyrics have been provided for selected pieces as a tool for aural learning, either through singing or speaking. Please take care in the use of lyrics for singing, as some of the pieces span ranges that may not be appropriate for all singing voices. Lyrics should not be used in the exam.

If you are preparing for an exam, please check www.trinitycollege.com/musictracks for the most up-to-date version of the syllabus, as this may change from time to time.

Group A
Film Music!

Film music helps show the thoughts, moods and intentions of the characters on screen, as well as adding greatly to the atmosphere of the film. Technically, film music was invented before dialogue – this is because films were originally silent, accompanied in the theatre by a live pianist or organist. Film music has changed a lot since then, with large orchestral soundtracks forming a vital part of most blockbuster films.

This piece conveys a range of different emotions. Can you imagine what might be happening on the screen in each section of this piece? Try to give each section a different feeling, using the details in the score – including dynamics, accents and slurring – to help emphasise the contrasts.

In the exam, you should play the repeated section as many times as there are learners in your group, so that everyone gets a chance to perform the solo section.

Small Group Tracks Violin – Track 2

Film Music!

Dramatic film music ♩ = 126

C Lawry

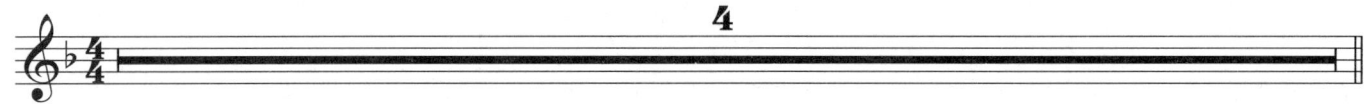

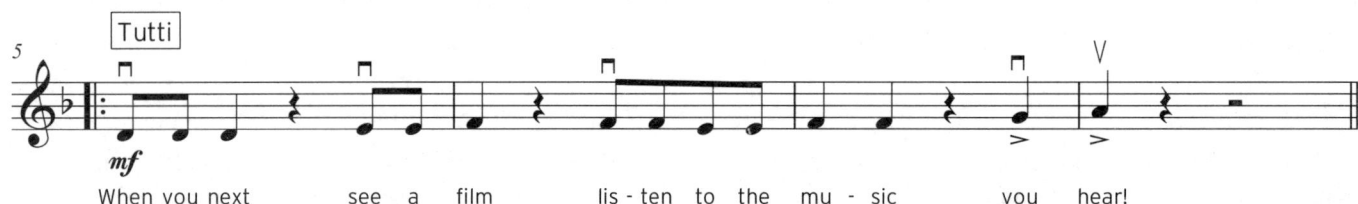

When you next see a film lis-ten to the mu-sic you hear!

There's a shad-ow in the dark-ness creep - ing, 'round the bed of some-one sound-ly sleep - ing!

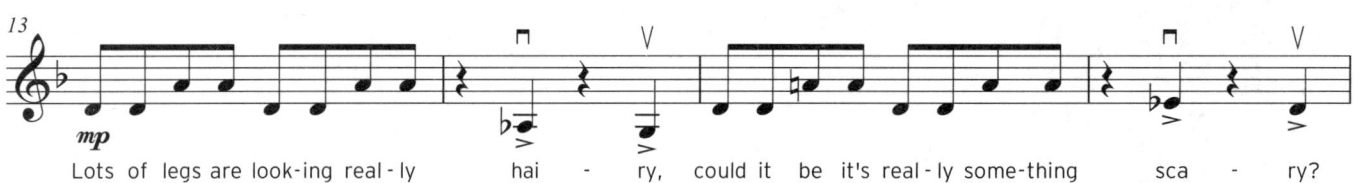

Lots of legs are look-ing real-ly hai - ry, could it be it's real-ly some-thing sca - ry?

When we hear the mu-sic change it might be that we're think-ing some-thing strange might hap-pen!

When the drums start to pound; a big dra-mat - ic sound!

25
mp
Mu - sic in films real - ly helps make it real, so
29
Repeat as necessary
mf
you real - ly feel what the act - ors will feel.
Tutti (last time only)
33
f
When you next see a film lis - ten to the mu - sic you hear!

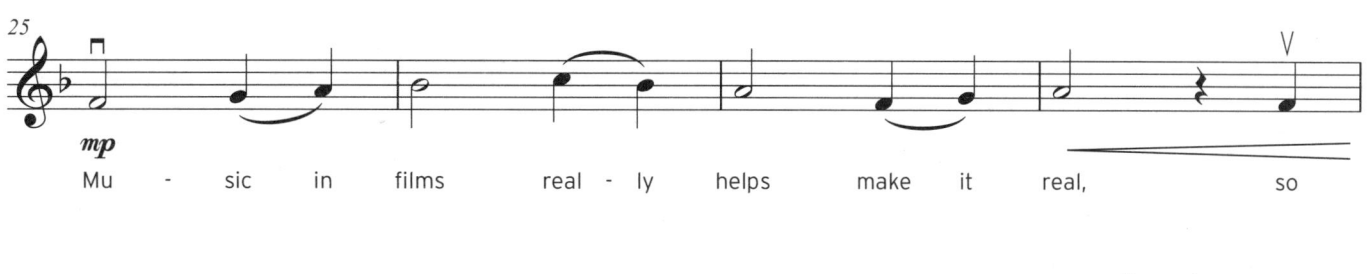

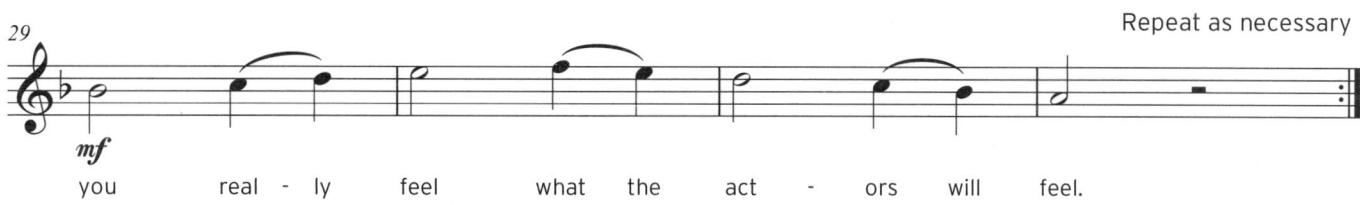

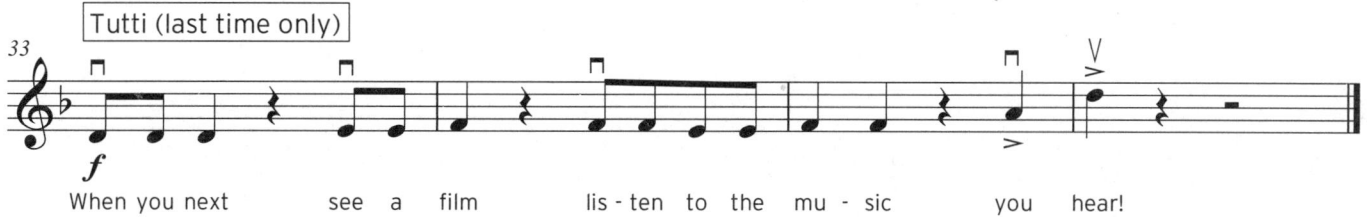

Group A
Vesper's Valse

Jazz is a varied genre of music that was born in America in the early 20th century. It has a lot of different influences, from African-American slave spirituals to European classical music. What makes it easy to recognise is its use of 'blue notes' - clashing notes that give a cool, expressive feeling - as well as swing rhythm, complex harmony and the use of improvisation. These features remain an important part of jazz as it continues to grow and evolve.

This piece is a jazz waltz - a dance with three beats in each bar. It's in the key of A major, so look out for those sharps! Practising your A major scale will help you get comfortable with some of the patterns in this piece. Be sure to follow the dynamics, which build to a loud climax at a point where some accidentals appear in the melody.

In the exam, you should play the repeated section as many times as there are learners in your group, so that everyone gets a chance to perform the solo section.

Vesper's Valse

Waltz ♩ = 104

D Foster

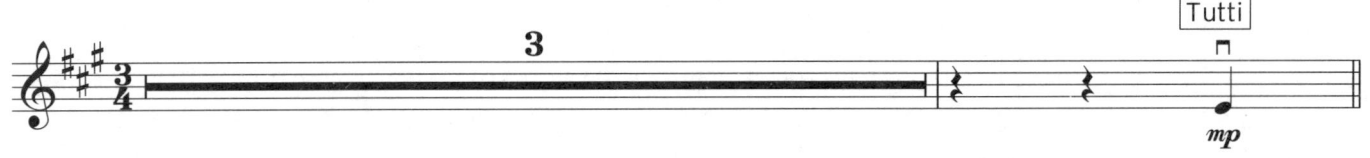

Group A
Midnight Carnival

Over 400 years ago, Portuguese traders sailed the world trading silk and spices. Thinking they were nearly home, they stumbled upon South America and loved it so much that they never left! **Samba** is a combination of music from these early Portuguese settlers, African slaves and influences of native folk music. It has a distinctive syncopated rhythm that evokes the spirit of colourful Brazilian carnivals.

Staccato and accents are an important part of this piece – these will help drive the rhythm along as well as bringing out the music's character. There are also some *crescendos* and *decrescendos* to look out for, which will add shape to your performance. See if you can keep your energy high, even in the quieter sections.

In the exam, you should play the repeated section as many times as there are learners in your group, so that everyone gets a chance to perform the solo section.

Small Group Tracks Violin – Track 2

Midnight Carnival

Tracks 8, 9, 10

Samba ♩ = 126

D Foster

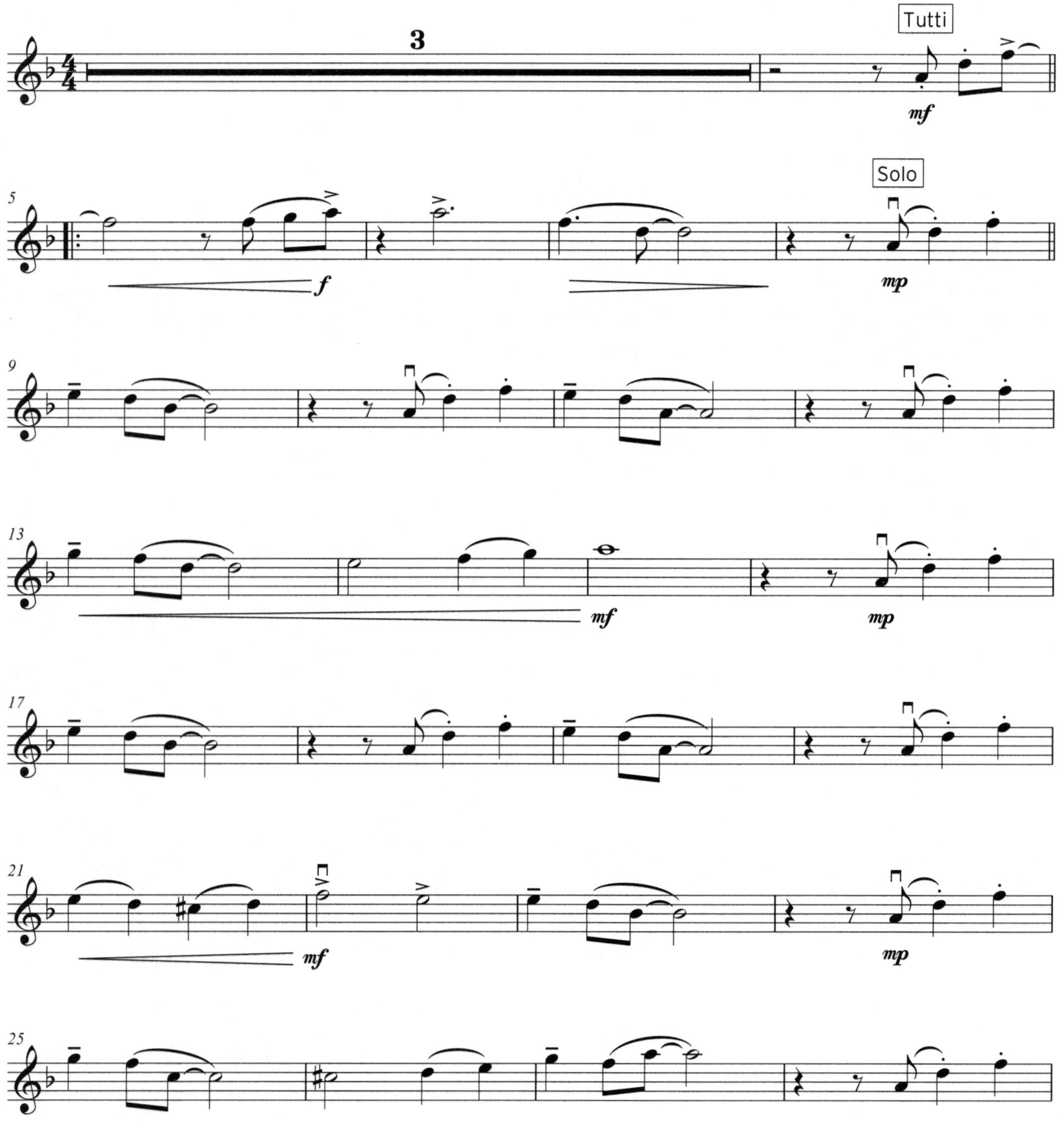

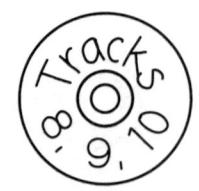

Group A
English Waltz

Folk music is the traditional music from any given country or region. English folk music goes back to when people started singing melodies, sometimes adding very simple accompaniments, perhaps with just a drum or a stringed instrument. Later, certain songs became popular and were used widely at special occasions, accompanied by larger groups of instruments.

This piece is reminiscent of waltzes that might have been played at public gatherings or dances. Try to capture a feeling of movement and dance in your performance, and look out for the *pizzicato* section in the middle. Towards the end there are some passages that feature an E minor broken chord, so practise your E minor arpeggio to feel comfortable with these shapes.

In the exam, you should play the repeated section as many times as there are learners in your group, so that everyone gets a chance to perform the solo section.

English Waltz

♩ = 112

A Podmore

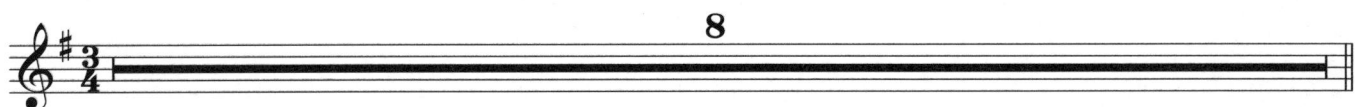

Dance___ in the dap - pled light! Sweep, Spring - tide sun, a - cross

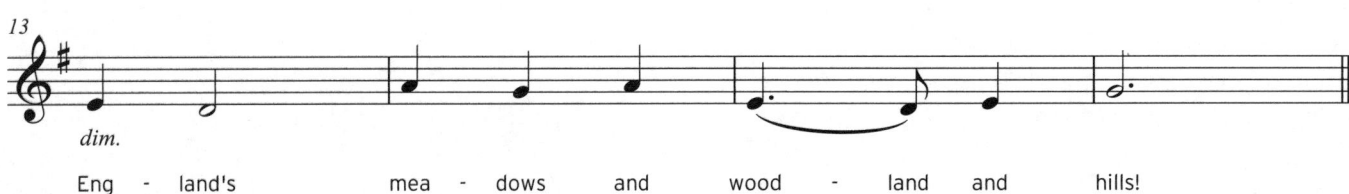

Eng - land's mea - dows and wood - land and hills!

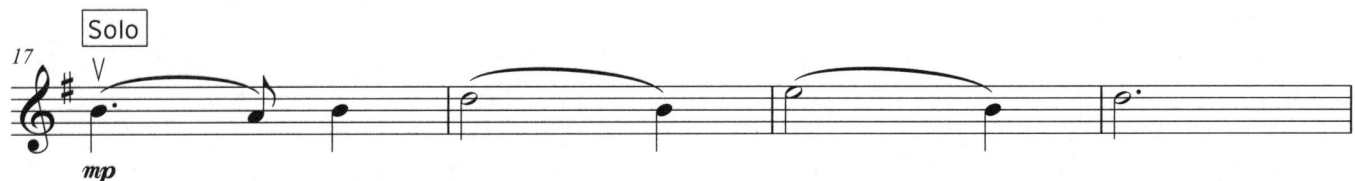

18 Trinity College London Copyright © 2014 Trinity College London. All rights reserved.

Group B – Technical Piece Pizzicato Delicato

The pieces in Group B are Technical Pieces. These have a different structure to Group A pieces, and a specific technical element has been identified for each one. It is important that you demonstrate this to the examiner when you perform your Technical Piece.

Technical Pieces are divided into four phrases, marked 1, 2, 3 and 4 on the score. In the exam, the examiner allocates a different phrase to each member of your group. You then perform the Technical Piece with each of you playing your allocated phrase. The phrases are not allocated in advance, so it is important that you learn the whole piece.

If there are two or three members in your group, the examiner allocates only the first two or three phrases and then stops the backing track after each of you has played. If there are four members, the examiner allocates all four phrases, and the group should also play the final *tutti* phrase together. The *tutti* phrase is not assessed, so don't worry if you don't get a chance to play it.

Technical element you will be assessed on in Pizzicato Delicato: pizzicato

The title of this piece is the clue to its technical focus. It is played *pizzicato* throughout, so you will need to show the examiner that you can pluck the strings in time with the pulse and with accurate rhythm. There is also a *crescendo* and a *decrescendo* in each phrase, so make sure that these dynamics come across in your *pizzicato*. This short piece is over in a flash, so try to make your performance accurate and effective right from the very first note!

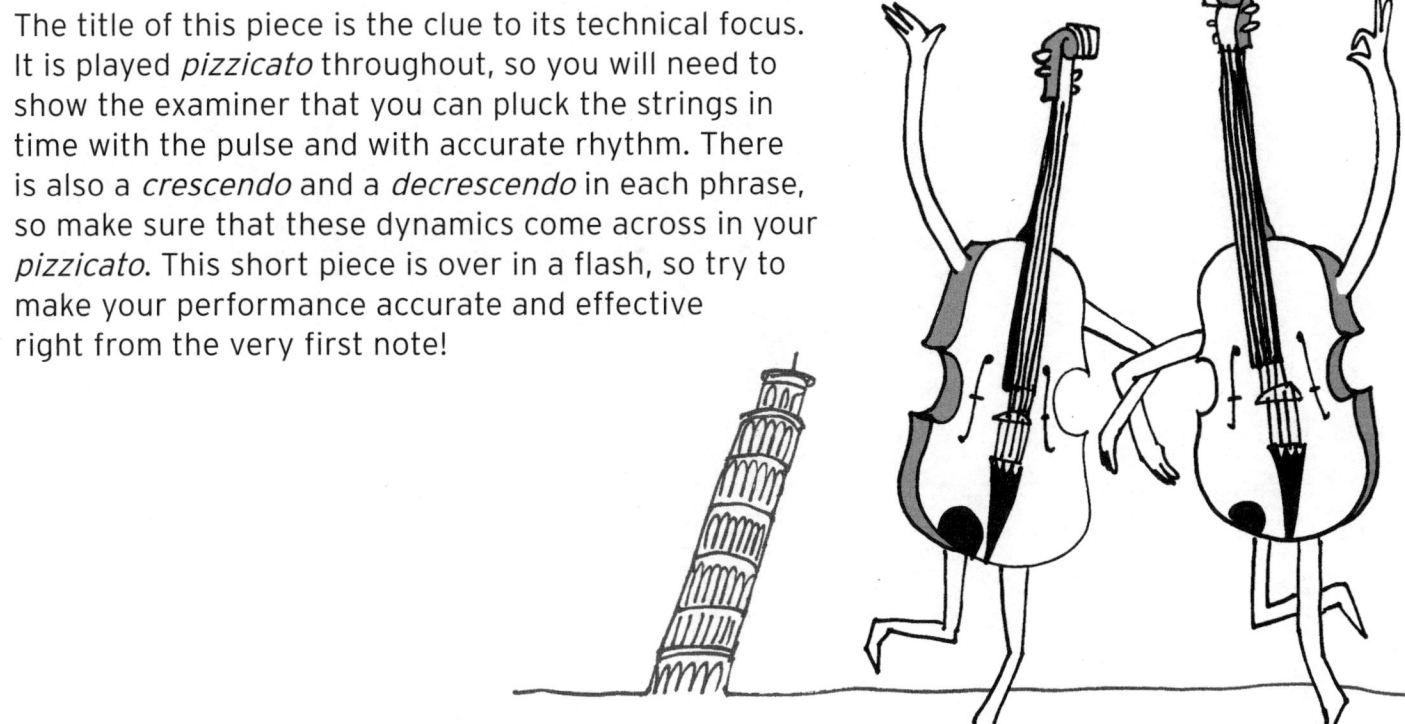

Small Group Tracks Violin – Track 2

Pizzicato Delicato

Italian folk dance ♩. = 80

C Lawry

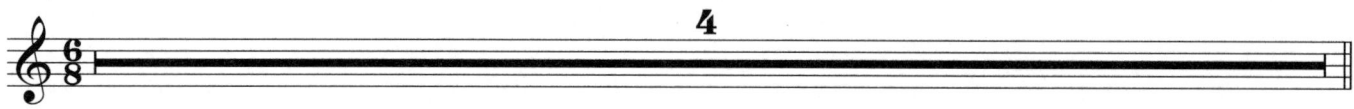

Group B - Technical Piece Who Needs Scales?

The pieces in Group B are Technical Pieces. These have a different structure to Group A pieces, and a specific technical element has been identified for each one. It is important that you demonstrate this to the examiner when you perform your Technical Piece.

Technical Pieces are divided into four phrases, marked 1, 2, 3 and 4 on the score. In the exam, the examiner allocates a different phrase to each member of your group. You then perform the Technical Piece with each of you playing your allocated phrase. The phrases are not allocated in advance, so it is important that you learn the whole piece.

If there are two or three members in your group, the examiner allocates only the first two or three phrases and then stops the backing track after each of you has played. If there are four members, the examiner allocates all four phrases, and the group should also play the final *tutti* phrase together. The *tutti* phrase is not assessed, so don't worry if you don't get a chance to play it.

Technical element you will be assessed on in Who Needs Scales: scalic passages

This piece has a simple rhythm and a melody containing lots of short sections of a D major scale. It might be an idea to practise your D major scale to familiarise yourself with the overall shape of the key before looking at the different scalic passages in this piece. The examiner will be listening out for these passages, so try to play them as evenly as you can and listen carefully to your tuning on each note – especially the occasional A sharps. If the title of the piece is a question you have ever asked, the lyrics might provide an answer!

Who Needs Scales?

Pop ballad ♩ = 73

A Hampton

The Musicianship Skills tests

Copyback

Your group must choose between **Copyback** and **Improvising** for the Musicianship Skills test. (Please note that the whole group must choose the same test.) **Copyback** involves taking it in turns to play along with a backing track, repeating four short musical phrases straight after you have heard each one. You will not have seen or heard the phrases before, but you will be familiar with the backing track – it will be taken from a piece in this book, or one very similar in style or genre.

In the exam, the examiner gives each member of your group a notated version of the phrases, and the group as a whole is given 30 seconds to study or try out the phrases. The examiner also gives the order in which the members of your group should perform the test. The group then performs the test twice: first time for practice and second time for assessment. The backing track runs throughout the test, and the examiner will start and stop it for both performances.

Over the page are some example tests. You can find backing tracks for the example tests on the CD in this book.

Note for teachers

The Copyback example tests have been provided as a guide to what the test will be like in the exam. Please note that the test in the exam will be different to these examples, with a different backing track.

You are advised to use the example tests with your learners to help familiarise them with the format of the test. Each example test contains material for four different candidates, so try assigning a different performance order to your learners each time you use the example tests.

Copyback - Example 1

Candidate 1

Listen 1st time, play 2nd time.

Candidate 2

Candidate 3

Candidate 4

30 Trinity College London

Copyright © 2014 Trinity College London. All rights reserved.

Copyback - Example 2

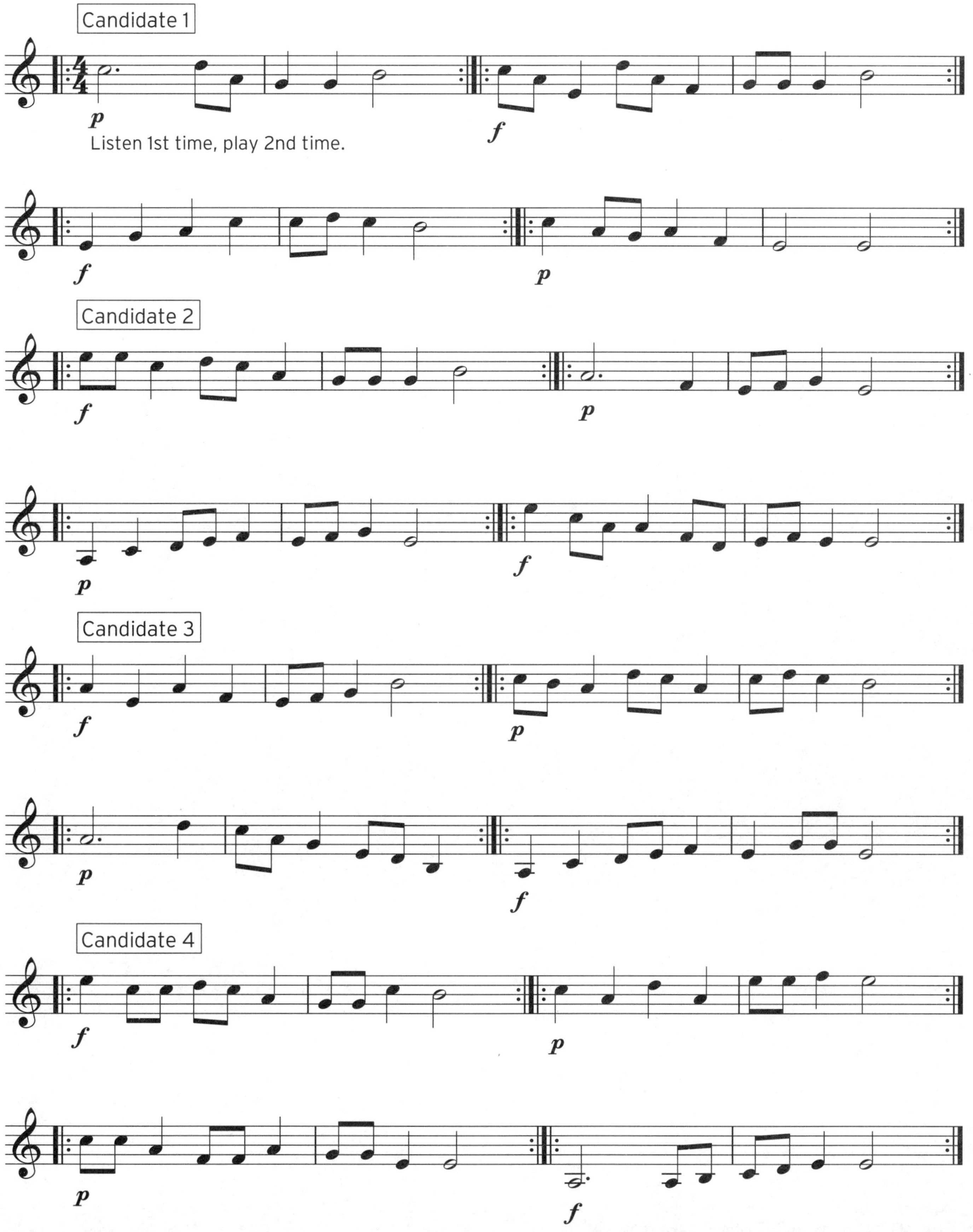

Candidate 1

Listen 1st time, play 2nd time.

Candidate 2

Candidate 3

Candidate 4

The Musicianship Skills tests

Improvising

The **Improvising** test involves taking it in turns to improvise over a backing track taken from a piece in this book, or one very similar in style or genre.

In the exam, the examiner gives each member of your group a chord chart and plays a few bars of the backing track to give you a sense of the tempo and feel. The group as a whole is then given 30 seconds to prepare and try out some ideas. Five pitches are suggested on the chord chart for you to use in your improvisation – you can choose to use these pitches, these and others, or a completely different set of pitches. You are free to discuss your choices with each other in the 30 seconds' preparation time, and your choices won't affect the marks you are given – you are marked purely on the quality of your improvisation, whichever notes you use.

The examiner gives the order in which the members of your group should perform the test. You then perform the test twice: first time for practice and second time for assessment. The examiner starts and stops the backing track for both performances, and also indicates when each of you should start and stop improvising. As a guide, each of you should improvise for about 16 bars.

Over the page are some example tests. You can find backing tracks for the example tests on the CD in this book.

Note for teachers

The backing tracks for the Improvising test are long loops of music, usually a repeating eight-bar chord sequence. To help learners know where they are in the music and structure their improvisations accordingly, the examiner will direct each learner to start improvising at the beginning of the chord sequence. This should be your guide when preparing learners for the Improvising test.

The backing tracks can also be used as a resource for different kinds of improvising, so try giving your learners different sets of pitches for them to experiment with. How do different stimuli affect their improvisations? You could also try developing their improvising skills by giving them rhythms instead of pitches, or even visual images.

Improvising - Example 1

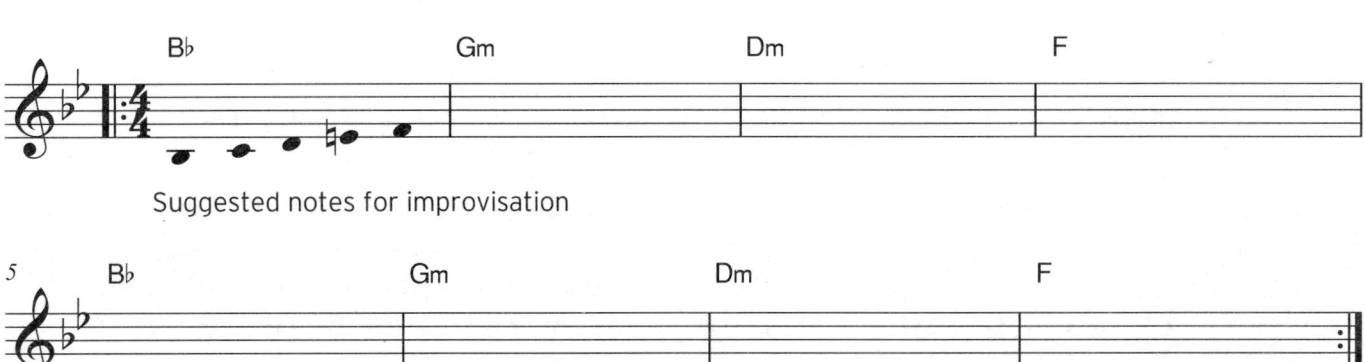

Suggested notes for improvisation

Improvising - Example 2

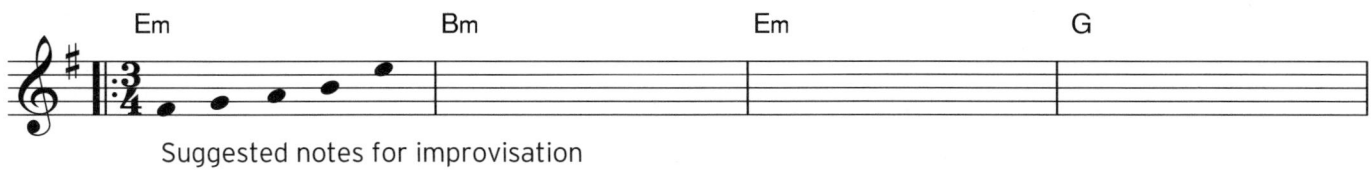

Suggested notes for improvisation

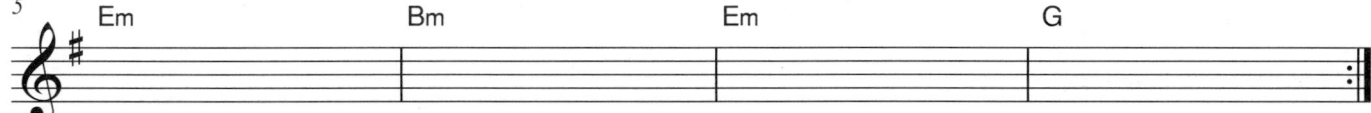

CD track listing

1 Tuning notes (G, D, A, E)
2 **Film Music!** (backing track - 2 candidates)
3 **Film Music!** (backing track - 3 candidates)
4 **Film Music!** (backing track - 4 candidates)
5 **Vesper's Valse** (backing track - 2 candidates)
6 **Vesper's Valse** (backing track - 3 candidates)
7 **Vesper's Valse** (backing track - 4 candidates)
8 **Midnight Carnival** (backing track - 2 candidates)
9 **Midnight Carnival** (backing track - 3 candidates)
10 **Midnight Carnival** (backing track - 4 candidates)
11 **English Waltz** (backing track - 2 candidates)
12 **English Waltz** (backing track - 3 candidates)
13 **English Waltz** (backing track - 4 candidates)
14 **Pizzicato Delicato** (backing track)
15 **Who Needs Scales?** (backing track)
16 Copyback - example 1 (backing track)
17 Copyback - example 2 (backing track)
18 Improvising - example 1 (backing track)
19 Improvising - example 2 (backing track)